ABOUT THE AUTHOR

At the age of 17, RoseMaree Templeton began to study the science of numbers. Her teacher and mentor was her grandmother, Hettie Templeton, who was the first Australian authority on the subject now more widely known as numerology. Hettie's first book on the subject was published in 1940.

RoseMaree has given numerous talks and lectures on numerology. She has also modified lessons for distance learning, held workshops and done countless readings. Her main objective is to help people live their lives more successfully in their everyday routine with the help of numerology and practical metaphysics.

RoseMaree lives in Sydney, Australia.

ROSEMAREE TEMPLETON

NUMEROLOGY ORACLE

R
ROCKPOOL

A Rockpool book
PO Box 252
Summer Hill
NSW 2130
Australia

rockpoolpublishing.com

Follow us! f ⊙ rockpoolpublishing
Tag your images with #rockpoolpublishing

ISBN: 9781922579539

Published in 2024 by Rockpool Publishing
Copyright text © RoseMaree Templeton 2024
Copyright design © Rockpool Publishing 2024

Design by Alissa Dinallo, Rockpool Publishing
Edited by Heather Millar

Printed and bound in China
10 9 8 7 6 5 4 3 2 1

CONTENTS

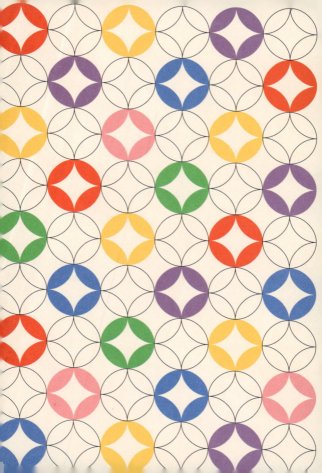

INTRODUCTION

A BRIEF OVERVIEW OF NUMEROLOGY

Pythagoras, the Greek philosopher and mathematician, who lived and died around 570–495 BCE, was also known as the Father of Numbers. Just who invented numbers, we shall never know. They were employed by the Arabs, who may have borrowed them from the Hindus. However, if we consult the numbers themselves, we are told they come from the gods.

According to Pythagoras, each number vibrates at a different speed, which gives the numbers their different meanings and personalities. In this way, the energy in the numbers can be translated to the human psyche.

Although Pythagoras did not invent numbers, he was certainly the father of number analysis. Everything, he believed, is numerical, and there is nothing that cannot be explained through numbers.

Some might ask, 'Where did Pythagoras get his knowledge and understanding?' or 'Where do such great people get their knowledge?' But when we consider the power of genius, these questions are unanswerable.

Pythagoras invented a technique that has served science for over 2,000 years. Mystical belief in the numbers pre-dates Christianity.

HOW THIS CARD DECK CAME ABOUT

Pythagoras based his teachings on mathematics, music and astronomy, stating that they are the basis of all the arts and sciences. He claimed mathematics to be the first law since it is possible for numbers to exist without music and astronomy, but nothing can exist without numbers.

Each being is aligned with the energy of a particular number, and this is how we are able to discern the interconnectedness of all things and see how everything that exists is connected to the same energy.

Just as our earth is a living, vibrating being, everything on it or in it is also living and vibrating at its own individual frequency. This includes our spirit friends – seen and unseen. As with all things in this universe, each of these spirit beings can be aligned with a number.

For many years, I have loved both the ascended masters and the archangels, since I was taught about them by the American spiritual leader and writer Elizabeth Clare Prophet. I have personally worked out the number for each ascended master and archangel in this card pack, according to the Pythagorean use of numbers and my own particular numerology methods. Each ascended master and archangel has their own role and energy, each also representing numbers. The advice you will receive comes from both the spiritual dimension as well as the meaning of the number, resulting in a more specific and personalised reading.

Knowing that Pythagoras believed 'all things are number' (his fundamental credo) and that numbers have personalities, I decided it might be a loving gesture to add some of these wonderful 'beings' to this numerology card deck. It is with this in mind, I have pleasure in presenting this deck of 36 reading cards, made up as follows:

- ✦ 14 numerology number cards, including the zero
- ✦ 4 karmic (serendipity) cards
- ✦ 8 abundance cards
- ✦ 5 archangel cards
- ✦ 5 ascended master cards.

The numbers in this deck have also been manually linked to colour and nature. For this reason, the cards have been illustrated with gorgeous emblems. Looking at the images complements the energy of the cards. This deck therefore offers a triple-reading, and potentially offers an ultra-personalised message. The energy of the images will warm your heart and work to provide a more specific reading.

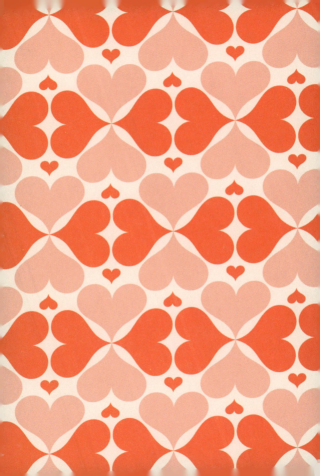

HOW TO USE THE CARDS

While holding the pack, before asking your question, close your eyes and sit quietly for a few moments, doing your best to still your mind while breathing calmly and evenly. When you feel ready and with your eyes still closed, begin shuffling the pack while asking for the energies of your particular guides to be with you.

With your eyes still closed, ask your question while continuing to shuffle the cards. If a card is dropped, pick it up and take a quick look to see if it relates to you in any way, then return it to the pack and continue shuffling.

Ask your question unambiguously – in other words, ask so that there is no doubt about what you are asking.

If there is a time when no question is asked, draw the card or cards, placing each one as directed in the card spreads section, and read the message offered.

If the card or cards drawn fail to give you an answer to the question you have asked, perhaps you are being given answers that better suit you at this time. So before you dismiss the words, think about them. Perhaps they are saying something you do not want to hear. If this is the situation, be deeply honest with yourself. Perhaps now is the time to recognise and admit a truth to yourself.

Sometimes the answers do not come because you asked carelessly or perhaps did not focus as closely as needed before you chose the cards. Do not be hasty. Again, read the words thoughtfully before dismissing them.

If you prefer shuffling again to have another spread, then do as your heart tells you.

If the same number is repeatedly drawn, take a closer look at why this is occurring. You might find this enquiry answers your question.

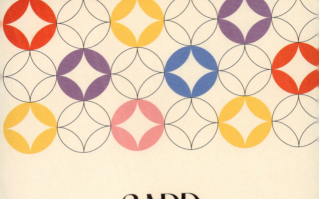

CARD
SPREADS

CARD OF THE DAY

Technique 1: Setting the vibration of the day

Only using the ascended masters and archangels cards, we can set the intention of the day by drawing a single card. Shuffle the cards and draw a single card from the top; shuffle the cards and cut the deck in half and draw the card from the top or bottom of the split pile; or shuffle the cards, fan the deck and choose one card.

Technique 2: Asking a question for the day ahead.

Using the entire deck of cards, shuffle the cards and ask your question. Spread the cards face down and choose one card.

TRINITY SPREAD

This spread is based on the triangle — a polygon with three sides. According to Aristotle, everything is bounded by threes, for everything has a beginning, a middle and an end. It also points to the direct connection between mind, body and soul — in other words, thinking, action and feeling — and also the inseparability of past, present and future.

Shuffle the cards. When ready, draw three cards, and place them in order of positioning.

- ✦ *Card 1*: 'you now' or the present
- ✦ *Card 2*: the past, or 'what is behind you'
- ✦ *Card 3*: the outcome or the future.

STAR SPREAD

The symbol of the Pythagoreans was the five-pointed star formed by drawing the diagonals of a regular pentagon. The pentagram, when upright, symbolises the five elements – earth, air, fire, water and spirit (the top point).

Shuffle the cards. As you draw the cards, place each one on the star in consecutive order, one at a time (as suggested below).

Place the first card on star point number 1, the second card on star point number 2, and so on till all five cards are placed.

+ *Card 1*: the query
+ *Card 2*: surrounding influences
+ *Card 3*: elements to consider
+ *Card 4*: possible solutions
+ *Card 5*: the outcome.

A SHORT MEDITATION

Sit in a spot where you will be
comfortable and not fidgety.

Close your eyes and relax.

Breathe deeply and evenly.

As you settle, your breathing
will become shallower.

Try not to think of the happenings of the
day or what you need to do tomorrow.

Imagine you are in a little boat drifting
gently along a beautiful river.

There is nothing to harm you.

The day is sunny and warm and the sun is
sparkling like jewels on the water.

You can see small birds flying above you
and hear them twittering in the trees.

The grass on the riverbanks is a lovely green.

And the leaves on the trees have wonderful
colours of green, red and yellow.

It is so very peaceful.

After a little while, bend your head
slightly over the side of the boat and look
deep into the water.

The water is crystal clear and you can see
all the way to the bottom of the river.

Down there, you can also see smooth
pebbles of all shapes and sizes.

There are small rainbow-coloured fish
swimming about.

Can you see them?

When you have finished looking into
the water, sit back in the boat and relax.

Stay in that relaxed condition,
drifting in the boat, feeling the warmth
of the sun for as long as you can.

When you have finished, step out of the boat and
feel the warm earth beneath your feet.

Feel your body becoming solid and grounded.

Slowly open your eyes.

NUMEROLOGY
CARDS

COMFORT

An open heart gives comfort and understanding. The zero is said to be a karmic number and can enter our lives at any time. For instance, the zero can enter our lives within the numbers of a birthday or the numbers in a name. We can liken the zero to love, for it too often has karmic attachments that can enter our lives at any time.

Love, like the zero, has no beginning and no end and is held in high regard by all creatures throughout our world.

In drawing the Love card you are lovingly urged to open your heart to universal love at this time – feel love's wonderful potential when you carry it within your heart.

Love is found in many places under many different names. Love is said to be one of the strongest powers in the world. Love is intangible – and it is known as a mystery. Love is where it falls and can be just around the corner.

Under whichever name we call it, it is true that all types of love can come into our lives at any time – and often when we least expect it.

The message this card brings is . . .
Let your love shine and see where it takes you.

INDIVIDUALITY

You have drawn the card of action, which indicates individuality, leadership and versatility. It is asking, what in your life needs attending to at this time? It is urging you to think – to be your own person. It often indicates a new beginning. This is a time to have courage and a time to act – not to stand back. Show your versatility; go it alone with an idea.

Knowledge and understanding are the keywords when endeavouring to gain ground. In this regard, there may be someone in the family, or perhaps a friend, who is looking to you for some type of guidance or plan. It is to your advantage that you make yourself available and show your willingness to help.

This number vibrates to the colour flame.

Whenever you need a little help, try wearing the colour flame in a garment or scarf or perhaps a tie or pocket handkerchief.

COOPERATION

This is the card of duality. Drawing this card indicates that now is not an independent time for you. This card tells you that this is a time to listen and cooperate. You are being advised to follow your own intuition, listen to the concerns of others, and be sure to use tact and diplomacy.

Drawing this card also indicates that you are looked upon for answers that will lead to a peaceful outcome and that you have now become the mediator and the light bearer. This is not a time for discord. Keep your positive purpose before you.

This number vibrates to gold.

It is believed to be the only colour impenetrable to the lower energy forces. To attract the desired energies so that you might help those in need, wear a piece of deep yellow clothing (suggesting gold) or perhaps a scarf, tie or pocket handkerchief with that colour in it. You could also wear some gold or gold-coloured jewellery.

CREATIVITY

If you have drawn this card, you are being asked to focus on giving help and understanding to someone who might need comfort at this time.

You are also required to be the optimist. Listening and passing on happy energy is called for now. Also, by using some creative way to do this would be of great benefit to the person needing your advice.

Maybe you could do with some happy energy yourself, and if this is the case, do your best to turn your thoughts to happy times.

This card also indicates opportunities and deals with feelings and inspiration. You are being advised to examine life on the broader scale because you are blessed with choice and prophecy and are asked to use your intuition. You are also lovingly urged to be tolerant with those around you.

This number resonates to the colours ruby, gold and amber.

To attract the desired energies closer to you, wear one or more of these colours. Perhaps you have a garment in these colours you can wear, or a scarf, tie or pocket handkerchief.

JUSTICE

The square symbolises the product of equals and signifies justice. This card indicates that eventually our dreams must have concrete form if they are to be realised.

In drawing this card, you are advised to be diligent and patient at this time, because circumstances indicate that plans and dreams cannot be hurried. Perhaps there is more work to be done, or maybe someone needs your practical help right now.

Have you given thought to stepping outside the box with your plans or dreams? This might be the time to do that. Also, this is not a time to be careless as this could bring adverse results. Think carefully – go through the process systematically.

To give you some variation, it would be a positive objective to turn your attention to someone who needs a friend right now.

If you are working hard in a positive way, you will have no need to feel dissatisfied.

This number vibrates to the colours green and blue

To attract some help when you need it, try wearing green or blue. Green expresses through the intellect, while blue seeks to express spiritual light.

EXPANSION

Drawing this card indicates that this is a time for you to be versatile, generous and to expand your thinking. Also, do your best to honour a promise you might have made – and forgotten.

This is also a card of change. Within your associations or close relationships, you need some freedom – mentally and physically – to progress. Be mindful of your words when explaining to someone about needing some freedom – a bit of time to yourself. Perhaps there are a few issues you'd like to consider that need clear thinking.

All life progresses through change and new ideas. By letting go of the old, the new can be realised. If you enjoy working within the public arena, this could be your opportunity to take the step forward.

You do not necessarily have to be a rolling stone gathering no moss, but do not be a procrastinator either.

This number vibrates to pink,
expressing power, life and love.

Wear pink in its various shades, either in a garment or a scarf, tie or pocket handkerchief when you need some help during this time.

REASONING

The double triangle overlaid symbolises thinking and reasoning. This card indicates that to be loved and to love unconditionally might be all you ask of family and friends. However, it is understood that to be appreciated for the little things we do for those we love goes a long way.

In drawing this card, you are reminded that you are loved and appreciated. You are being urged at this time to continue giving comfort where needed, because you are the comforter and you are loved in return. Home and family are nothing without the comforter.

If appreciation does not appear to be forthcoming, try not to allow that to hurt your heart. Take comfort in knowing that within each of us we have all the love in the world we will ever need. Perhaps knowing this might give some loving comfort to you.

This number vibrates to orange, scarlet and heliotrope (a pink-purplish colour).

It shows power, maternity and love for humanity. Wearing a garment, tie or pocket handkerchief in these colours will assist if you need help in realising unconditional love.

UNDERSTANDING

The number 7 is known as the temple, and its symbol is a triangle sitting on top of a square. This symbol resonates with mysticism and idealism, plus illusion and disillusion.

In drawing this card, you are reminded that knowledge is power. What is there in your life right now that requires you to gather knowledge? The more you know, the more success will follow.

Use the inner power that you feel right now to inspire others – whether it is in friendship or business. If you listen to your inner guidance, you have nothing to fear.

Learn to be pliable with listening and understanding. This is not a time to be unwilling. Be determined in a positive way.

If, within yourself right now, you feel that you'd like some uninterrupted 'me time', then allow yourself to do that, making sure you inform family and close friends of your intention. This feeling of isolation shouldn't last long and you'll be your old self in no time.

This number vibrates to the colours
purple, pearl, old rose and magenta.

Wear one or more of these colours when you feel you need a boost.

POWERFUL ENERGY

The two circles symbolise two worlds the spiritual and the material. The two squares symbolise independence. The two triangles symbolise the hourglass – the balance of cause and effect.

Drawing this card indicates there is a strong power with you – and because this is thought of as a karmic number, fate can turn either way. Show your desire to be unselfish, true and honest at this time and success could be yours.

You might be feeling independent right now, and this might cause misunderstandings with family or friends. Show your dependability, as a friend to others, either by putting your feelings into words, buying a gift or doing a good deed.

When success is imminent for you, claim it – this is not the time to sabotage your hard work.

This number has the meaning of a new higher cycle, which vibrates to canary and opal colours.

Wearing a garment with any of these colours should help boost your present cause. You might also wear them in a scarf or tie.

COMPASSION

This card is universal and can bring many things to you, including an overall awareness. It could be a time in your life when something is ending, making way for a new beginning. Be sure to stay positive. You are also being asked to think of others and to show your humility. Also, it is to your advantage to forgive where necessary or to ask for forgiveness.

Drawing this card means, if you are asked for help, you should do your best to assist any way you can. Be just in all you do, for right now you are the humanitarian, and you are also urged to show universal love towards all living things.

An indicator for this card is for imagination – as well as romance – to enter your life.

This number vibrates to red, beige (or light brown) and sometimes blue or green.

If you have garments or accessories of these colours in your wardrobe, it will be a great help towards meeting your goals if you wear them during this time.

LEADERSHIP

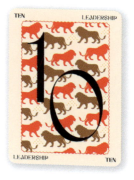

The number 10 stands for unity and creation. The symbol on this card suggests the Pythagorean *tetraktys* – or sacred decad. It consists of ten dots arranged in four rows.

Drawing this card indicates that using leadership qualities right now would be beneficial. You are also urged to be independent in your thinking on certain issues at this time. Perhaps you have an ambition to do something inspiring.

Also, while being independent in your thinking, it would be a positive move to be adaptable in certain situations.

If you are doing something that takes courage or you are worried that you might fail, take heart and know that drawing this card gives you strength to carry through and bring to fruition that which is in your heart.

So that your own dominance does not hinder your goals of leadership and ambition, be always mindful of how you go about gaining those qualities.

This number vibrates to flame and colours of the earth.

If you have a garment made of these colours, wear it at this time.

SPIRITUAL MESSENGER

This spiritual messenger asks that you use your intuition to be of help. It indicates that there are those needing more than material help at this time in a certain situation. Since this is the case, be positive and constructive when offering your help, remembering to be friendly and cooperative too.

Love of refinement and beauty are gracious, but right now you are the spiritual messenger, needed to give advice in a loving and caring way.

Drawing this card is letting you know that help from the universe is at hand – you only have to ask. Hopefully, the universe will offer a thought to you to be put forward to the ones you are helping – a stroke of genius perhaps.

This number vibrates to the colours
white, violet, yellow and black.

They show the complete cycle from light to darkness.

During this vital time of asking for help, and to enable you in turn to offer help, wear one or more of the above colours. You might have garments in your wardrobe in these colours, or perhaps you could wear a suitable scarf, tie or pocket handkerchief.

Please note – black, when considered in a positive way, is protective.

SPIRITUAL UNDERSTANDING

This is a card of spiritual understanding and big responsibility – know you are worthy of these deeds. Be calm, be a charming friend and be kind to the helpless, allowing your spiritual understanding to shine through. Be all these things while carrying your responsibility, and most of all, show that you are dependable.

Drawing this card indicates that perhaps there is a situation where something must be said. Now is the time for you to find a voice and speak what is on your mind.

There are times when we must look beyond the material to be of help.

Do your best to find the balance between the spiritual and the material because there you will find not only what you are looking for, you will also find joy in your life.

This number vibrates to the colour
cream and means cooperation.

It has the power to join the material and spiritual and to understand what unity means.

Wear the colour cream when you feel you need some help. Perhaps you have a garment in cream, or a scarf, tie or pocket handkerchief.

THE TEACHER

Right now, you have the opportunity to be the teacher. Do not doubt yourself – there is strong, positive and unusual energy around you, giving you the courage to not doubt.

Drawing this card tells you the world is not perfect. People are not perfect. So do your best not to be upset by their actions. Seek to understand that, instead of looking for perfection, life will have more meaning when you realise what is needed from you is to give a message and feeling of inspiration in your everyday conversation when speaking with someone.

If there is a goal in your sights, be sure to make your way by working the necessary steps to reach that goal. Take your time because, if you hurry, mistakes will be made and is not your aim.

This card is urging you to have faith in yourself.

This number vibrates to orange, scarlet and heliotrope (a pink-purplish colour), showing power and love for humanity.

It would be helpful at this time to wear one or more of these colours in a garment, scarf, tie or pocket handkerchief.

KARMIC CARDS

The most commonly talked about karmic numbers are 13, 14, 16 and 19, and in this 36-card pack, some information has been written on each of these four numbers. These numbers offer specific lessons, which can be either positive or negative – and are personal to you.

When a karmic number pops up on a person's birthday or in another prominent area in their life, it is considered that a karmic debt must be paid in this life. The debt is here to teach and keep teaching until the person becomes aware that something in their life must change if they expect it to run smoothly. 'If you always do what you've always done, don't expect a different result.' I believe Henry Ford said it first.

INTUITION

Throughout many parts of the world the number 13 is often viewed as a bad omen owing to the fact there were 13 seated at the table at the Last Supper. Others view 13 as extremely propitious.

You have chosen this card because you are being asked to use the energy of the number 13 in the positive and blow away the part of it that is negative.

The message here is that you are urged to look at your life as a whole and also at sections of your present pathway. This card is telling you that you

 50

might be placing blame where it should not go. There are times when we all should turn the mirror to view our own reflection.

Perhaps there are areas in your life where things keep going wrong. This card is asking for understanding. Always look at your own shortcomings first, meeting those challenges with positive energy and strength. This will set you free to stand up and be responsible, and will also enable you to find happiness in something you will eventually realise as truth.

Drawing this card indicates you could be suppressing your desire to express yourself freely, and you could be feeling very highly strung right now. This is a time to have faith, not self-doubt.

With wisdom comes power.

BALANCE

In drawing this card, you are being urged to put balance back into your life.

This number initially stands for order and emotional stability and being able to adjust to quick-changing issues that turn up without notice. In the meantime, you are most likely dealing with ordinary everyday occurrences, such as work and what is going on at home. Life might feel a bit like a juggling act right now.

Several famous people throughout history, including Cicero, Pythagoras and Ralph Waldo Emerson, are noted for the saying 'Moderation in all things' – or 'Never go to excess, but let moderation be your guide.' These famous sayings still stand strongly in today's philosophy.

If you are not injecting balance and moderation into your life, your life might not be as you want it to be. If you find you are indulging in certain interests and would like to change, drawing this card might hold the answer. Perhaps you would like to call on the Ascended Masters Serapis Bey, Lady Mary and El Morya. Choose one or speak to all three – see pages 90, 92 and 98.

What is there in your life at this time that you might be reluctant to commit to? It might be time to examine this area, and if you haven't already done so, look for ways to turn things around, because this could be delaying any effort to move forward.

Do your best to settle down with discipline and stay with it.

KNOWLEDGE

Drawing this card indicates that sudden happenings could present themselves in your life. To offer help, note there is wisdom to be found in the 7, which is the addition of 1 and 6.

Look at it this way: these changes are taking you the way you were meant to go for your best outcome, rather than the path you preferred, and for a while you might feel as though you are on a rollercoaster.

If you get the feeling that your life is crumbling, do not despair, for this is merely the old making way for something new — and for something better. You are urged to take a positive viewpoint, remembering to have faith in the universe, and know that there is always something good just around the corner.

Perhaps right now you feel you would like to have more time to yourself for a while. Just make sure you tell your family or friends that this is your intention — and take that time for yourself. Everybody needs to have a certain amount of 'me time'.

Drawing this card is telling you that when you meet your experiences in a positive and philosophical way, your intuition strengthens and deep understanding will be your reward.

DEVELOPMENT

If you have drawn this card, you are being urged to take a stand for self-development and self-realisation. This is a time to show courage and determination. Also, learn to cultivate your will and show your initiative and your individuality to bring forward your talents.

For yourself as well as others, stand positive.

The advice this card offers is that, if defeatism drives your actions, there could be difficulty in finding success and happiness in the outcome.

Perhaps there is an issue at the moment where you could think of the other person before yourself? You are advised to show tolerance and compassion in all situations right now. This might mean a personal struggle for you, but working through this will certainly be a feather in your cap – and the pride you feel will be most deserving.

If this is achieved it will bring happiness, which can be claimed as yours. This is self-earned happiness, and no-one has the right to take it from you.

If you are being offered help or advice in any form, then for your own sake, give strong thought to accepting it. This is one way of overcoming your past resistance in this area. Reach out to others, and you will find they will respond to you with love.

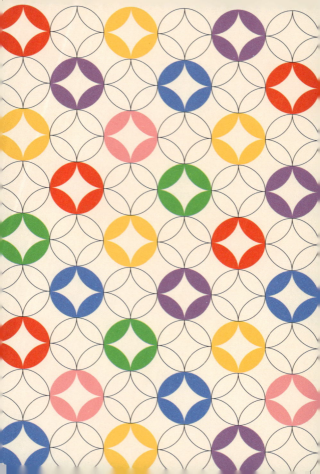

ABUNDANCE CARDS

What is abundance? It often means different things to different people. Some believe it's not what we have, it's what we are.

Others might believe it's a sense of something missing — a lack of something — because they haven't got what they want in abundance.

Yet some others might say they are abundantly grateful for what they have.

THE GREEN ROSE

Renewal

The green rose suggests renewal of life, rejuvenation and joyfulness. Life must always have change to evolve, and drawing this card indicates that change might be close at hand for you.

Green is an indication of growth, richness, plenty, balance and calm. Green is also a great help when someone is recovering from an illness, and it is said to be uplifting to the spirit.

Drawing this card usually suggests financial success, but this could be inconsistent. It is suggested that you maintain your focus and continue to be positive. To help you accomplish this, you are advised to take five to ten minutes from your day to sit quietly and meditate.

Ask your special guides to help keep you focused and be disciplined on your pathway of success. Afterwards, give loving thanks to your guides.

If you do not have a special guide, you might like to call on Ascended Master Serapis Bey – see page 92. Look for and feel the colour green while meditating.

To offer help when needed, you might like to wear various shades of green, including the colour turquoise, which is a mixture of blue and green.

GOLDEN LAUGHING BUDDHA

Focus

The golden laughing buddha is meant to bring abundance and happiness and is found in many homes, places of business, restaurants and more. He usually wears a robe, and he might wear beads, known as the 'pearls of wisdom'.

Keep the golden laughing buddha on your altar or somewhere within easy reach so that you and other members of your family can rub his tummy daily for wishes to be granted, happiness, problems to be solved and abundance in all things.

The golden buddha is not to be placed directly on the ground because this is considered disrespectful.

Buddha can be used in the home or in the garden and also for feng shui.

Always place the buddha facing your home for great abundance.

Drawing this card suggests work and discipline. However, be ever mindful that work and a correct line of thinking help money mount up and can bring in a golden nest egg.

This card is kindly reminding you that it is necessary to focus and to work diligently for what you want. However, along the pathway, remember to be thoughtful and have respect for yourself and others.

To offer help when needed, wear the colours blue or green.

BLUE SWIRL WITH PEARL

Wildcard

Abundance comes in many different forms and is not always related to money.

Drawing this card suggests a) working hard for what you want b) a windfall c) an unexpected surprise. If you are a person who stays focused or you are the practical type, you will stick with the path of working for what you want out of life.

Finances could be a bit of a wildcard because this card suggests possibilities are there for you to draw large amounts of money to you, whether earned or through a windfall, as mentioned above. Avoid high-risk ventures that could be inclined to work against your chances of financial success. If you are wise and take a business approach, your finances could accumulate.

If you already have wonderful abundance in your life in whatever form, give thanks for it and for the abundance of knowledge you have obtained.

To gain help if needed, wear the colours purple, pearl or deep red.

If you have selected this card and you were born on a 22 day, there is a good chance you could do well in real estate.

PINK ROSE

Be thrifty

Pink roses signify love, romance, elegance and happiness, and silently bring with them the desired emotions. A very pale pink rose suggests calmness and sophistication. Roses are a gift for every occasion, not just St Valentine's Day when even a single rose can convey a thousand words to a loved one.

Each shade of pink conveys its own unique significance, which in turn is understood by the recipient. These magnificent roses bring joy to all who receive them, and such delight causes a rippling effect that spreads to those around them.

Drawing this card shows you that there is gratitude around you and you are being thanked for your kindness.

You are being guided to discipline yourself at this time to focus on how you are spending your money. In other words, do your best not to spend unnecessarily. This card is guiding you towards the understanding that following these suggestions will bring prosperity.

If you wish to draw on help from the universe, wear the colours blue, green and any shade of pink.

If you have chosen this card and you were born on an 11 day, you could have attributes such as seeing and knowing many things that other people fail to notice.

CHERRY BLOSSOMS

Joy

Cherry blossoms are symbolic of renewal and the delicate nature of life. They suggest life, joy and happiness, and while they are in bloom, there is celebration beneath the cherry blossom trees. This is the Japanese custom of 'hanami', which means 'watching blossoms'.

Drawing this card suggests that depending on your positive or negative beliefs and attitudes, there could either be good fortune in your future or just the opposite. Do your utmost not to give into thoughts that could bring you down.

There is the possibility that you can earn money in the corporate world. Also, it is suggested that you are most likely good at dealing with money. Perhaps it is with other people's money, such as being a banker or financial advisor.

If you deal with your own money, remain positive and have no fear of failure, and you will have success. Be aware that there is much power in having faith in yourself, otherwise you will fail because of self-sabotage. So think carefully – which road would you rather choose?

To gain help if you need it, wear the colours of the cherry blossoms – pink shades or opal.

MONEY TREE

Midas touch

The feng shui money tree is used as a symbol to attract wealth and prosperity and the plant most often used to represent this is the succulent jade. Once you have chosen your plant, there are many ways to place it. One of the simplest methods is to stand it either side of the outside of your front door. Make sure your front door is clear and the entrance is not blocked.

Drawing this card suggests that in most cases you have the ability to attract money effortlessly. However, it might slip through your fingers just as effortlessly if you fail to be disciplined in your spending.

It often leaves us with a 'feel-good' feeling when we buy gifts for others, but we must first make sure we can financially afford to do this before we part with our money.

But wait – perhaps you have what is called the 'Midas touch' and you know how to earn money and, importantly, you know how to save it and also when to spend it.

If you feel that you need a little help, try wearing the colours orange, red or gold – or, alternatively, try a pastel shade.

CORN

Advantage

In the positive, the symbol of corn is generally associated with abundance and plenty, including financial success. To dream of corn often means you are about to have success, which will bring financial opportunities.

In the negative, corn in a dream could mean your lack of concern about wasting hard-earned money. This is a warning about the need to take care of your money, and not to be wasteful or careless with it.

Drawing this card means you have a strong money-making advantage, and there is a possibility that this could be of benefit in bringing about a comfortable lifestyle. If this is your wish, work towards it with positive energy.

There could be 'karmic timing' attached to this card, whereby should there be a breakdown, failure or disappointment, bringing with it loss of money, you may be given the opportunity to begin again, having learnt a good lesson.

To offer help when needed, wear the colours flame or golden yellow – or, alternatively, try wearing blue, green or mauve.

LOTUS WITH FISH

Be pro-active

The lotus is a symbol of being able to rise from the murky waters of life into something beautiful. The lotus is said to symbolise purity and rebirth. Chinese philosopher Confucius was known to say, 'While growing in mud the lotus remains unstained.' A person's pathway in life can be likened to that of the lotus.

Lotus with fish is said to be more propitious.

Drawing this card suggests financial abundance either by way of working hard for your money or through an inheritance.

It is kindly suggested that you don't bide your time waiting for opportunities, but work diligently, hopefully loving what you do and keeping busy.

Sometimes looking at certain situations in life can be likened to standing on a hilltop surveying everything below and to the horizon, in that it puts things in perspective – and always helps us to see things more openly and clearly.

To gain help if needed, wear the colours cream, orange, red or purple.

If you were born on an 11 day or a 22 day, there is the possibility that energies drawn from this card could be doubled.

ARCHANGEL CARDS

An archangel is an angel of high rank who has gained this position, and an angel is a messenger who can influence people in making decisions.

Archangels are called protectors of all humanity. These beings can be called upon to protect and help in finding solutions for humanity, and at times they might appear in human form.

It is said that archangels 'supervise' the other angels who are not as high a rank. These great beings cannot intervene directly in our lives because of the universal law that we have free will. This is knowledge that has always been known to us. These spirit beings come to us when called to watch over us and to give comfort.

ARCHANGEL RAPHAEL

The healer

Archangel Raphael assists with healing humans – and animals. He heals the body, mind and spirit.

Drawing this card reminds you that if someone you know or a beloved pet needs healing to call on this archangel for assistance. You are also lovingly reminded that these special enlightened beings cannot interfere with free will, therefore any decision to accept or refuse help is up to you.

Archangel Raphael is also known as the patron of travellers, so if it is your wish, call on this wonderful archangel any time you are travelling.

Archangel Raphael is kind and loving, and you will know he's around when you feel or see flashes or sparkles of beautiful green light.

Call on this enlightened being when you feel the need.

ARCHANGEL GABRIEL

The communicator

Archangel Gabriel is known as the messenger of God. This enlightened being helps with advice and guidance to help organise your life, and is the angel for education and career. Gabriel can also help you find your life's purpose and have fulfilment. So if you are in need of advice and guidance at this time, call on Archangel Gabriel.

Drawing this card helps to inspire harmony if there is conflict around you. Or perhaps you would like to say something to someone and do not quite know how to say it. Call on this wonderful enlightened being for help.

Archangel Gabriel's colours are white, gold and citrine,
which is the colour of her stone.

ARCHANGEL MICHAEL

The protector

You have drawn the card of Archangel Michael. He often appears in a suit of silver armour, carrying a sword used to cut free the bonds that hold and bind us to the lower energies.

If you are unsure which direction to take at this time or if your spirits are low, Archangel Michael is once again there to help – to lift you and to give support and comfort.

Michael's powers are such that he can also be called upon when there's trouble with something mechanical or electrical, including computers.

If you draw this card, you are urged to call on beloved Archangel Michael if you need help or protection at any time.

Archangel Michael's colours are beautiful bright blue and purple, so if he's around you might see sparkles or flashes of these colours.

ARCHANGEL ZADKIEL

Forgiveness

Archangel Zadkiel provides positive energies, replacing negative energies with compassion and faith. In drawing this card, you are lovingly asked to forgive yourself and anyone who might need your forgiveness – likewise, ask others to forgive you. Forgiveness is twofold – it wipes clean burdens we carry in our hearts and souls towards another person or situation, and those we have forgiven can likewise feel the burden lifted. This does not mean we condone what we see as bad behaviour. It means that it is now time to hand the burden over to the great universe. Note that you can ask for forgiveness for yourself or help with forgiving others through prayer or meditation.

Archangel Zadkiel helps heal relationships with our self and with others and hurtfulness within the heart. He also asks that you be mindful that some relationships cannot be mended.

When you feel the need, call on this enlightened being.

Archangel Zadkiel's energy colours are shades of lavender, violet and indigo.

ARCHANGEL URIEL

The problem solver

Archangel Uriel helps with solving problems in everyday situations. He also brings in the power of unconditional forgiveness.

Archangel Uriel is known as the light of God, angel of wisdom and miracles, thoughts and ideas, creativity and astrology – just to name a few.

If you have drawn this card, Archangel Uriel is telling you that blessings can be found in adversity and offers help with turning your disappointments into victories. So if at this time you are faced with a hurtful situation, call on Uriel. This enlightened being will help to purify mental and emotional understanding.

He is here to help with manifesting positive thoughts to help bring our dreams – and thought-forms – to life.

Archangel Uriel's stone is amber and his colour is a deep golden yellow.

Wear this sunshine colour when you need to attract him. Call on him when you feel the need.

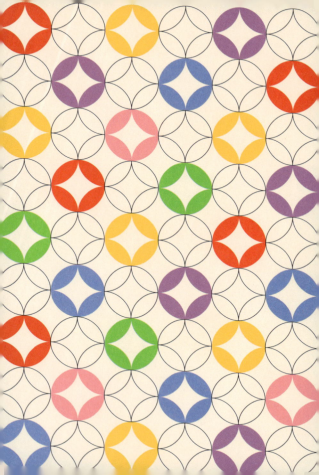

ASCENDED MASTER CARDS

Ascended masters, having experienced the spiritual growth of many lifetimes, possess the ability to assist in the uplifting of humanity by increasing the existing awareness of the spiritual energy that charges the universe.

Ascended masters are enlightened beings who work with us, showing us the way to peace and enlightenment. They are called the 'Great White Brotherhood/Sisterhood'. The colour white refers to the brilliant white light that accompanies these wonderful beings. They also each have their own colours by which they are known.

The energy of the ascended masters is matched to the energy of the numbers, so when you select a card you are getting a double reading. Each has a role to play in the card deck.

ASCENDED MASTER LADY MARY

Gentle energy

In drawing this card you have the influence of Lady Mary around you at this time and she will be strongly felt if you are seeking to express yourself in any manner. If disharmony is around you at the moment, you might feel gentle energy within you, as you take the role of the diplomat. Lady Mary also seeks to encourage adaptability and cooperation in other areas of your life.

If you fear criticism, you might hold back from speaking or acting on your own truth, but show the positive moon side of Lady Mary and go forward. She is leading you to the altar of your own heart and your own divinity.

Talk to Lady Mary and tell her your feelings of happiness, sadness or despair. Her energy is so gentle that when you feel its warmth surrounding you, it sometimes brings tears. Master Lady Mary is also known as Queen of the Angels.

ASCENDED MASTER SERAPIS BEY

Motivation

If you have drawn the card of Master Serapis Bey, who is influenced by the planet Mercury, you are being asked at this time to be prepared to learn some self-discipline. If you are willing to do this, you will be rewarded because of it.

The energy of Master Serapis Bey is with you now because he likes to motivate those who might need help with physical fitness and a healthy lifestyle.

To accept his offer of help, wear his colour — green — or if you see objects of green at this time, know that Master Serapis Bey is around you.

Call on Master Serapis Bey to help in your quest for self-discipline.

ASCENDED MASTER KUTHUMI

Responsibility

You have drawn the card of Ascended Master Kuthumi. He asks you at this time to accept the responsibilities that arise in the area of personal relationships. He also asks that you endeavour to understand unconditional love and non-judgement. The Master knows that this area of life is not an easy pathway. However, he lovingly urges you to always do your best to think and act with compassion. Self-discipline in this area will help enormously in your search for self-awareness.

This illuminated being is an initiate of love and wisdom. His symbol is the six-pointed star, and he is aligned with the state of joy.

Ascended Master Kuthumi's colours are
soft lemon and deep blue.

ASCENDED MASTER LADY KUAN YIN

Emotional healing

You have drawn the card of Ascended Master Lady Kuan Yin, master of unconditional love. She is known as the goddess of compassion and the bodhisattva of mercy. Kuan Yin is a great healer and works to heal the emotional body. She believes that it is from the emotions that much of our illnesses have their causes. Kuan Yin is here now to help clear any emotional issues, as well as any anger you might be experiencing.

Master Kuan Yin is known as 'she who hears prayers'. Pray to her or call upon her for help and also when you need protection.

Kuan Yin has a special affiliation with children, and her element is water.

Kuan Yin's colours are deep magenta and soft pink.

Her name can be spelt several ways: Kuan Yin, Kwan Yin, Quan Yin. She also answers to several names: Quan Am, Yin Guanin, Guanyin Quan, Kannon, Kamin and Kuannon. Calling the beloved Kuan Yin's name is sufficient for her to hear your prayers.

ASCENDED MASTER
EL MORYA

Self-discipline

In drawing this card you have the influence of the Master El Morya right now. The Master encourages you to strengthen your willpower. He urges planet Uranus to bring forth its influence to assist with this and also to help give you patience when needed.

Be mindful that Master El Morya is a hard taskmaster. It could be that you must decide either to keep to your present pathway or take the other fork in the road – that of self-discipline. Whichever path you take, remember to work hard and always be true to yourself.

If you need assistance with issues of willpower, patience and self-discipline at this time, call on Master El Morya.

The Master El Morya's colours
are violet and amethyst – sometimes blue.

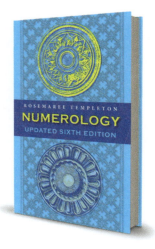

ISBN: 9781925429022
Available from all good book stores

NUMEROLOGY

UPDATED SIXTH EDITION

Numerologist RoseMaree Templeton combines the teachings of her renowned grandmother, Hettie Templeton, with her own insights and experience in this easy-to-understand book for both beginners and serious students.

The clear explanations show how to calculate and interpret the ruling number, day number, destiny number and personal year number for yourself, your family members and your friends. Learn how to draw up and read birthdate and name charts, arrows, and the pyramid charts that map peaks and troughs throughout the course of a lifetime.

The book also includes fascinating readings for well-known figures.